Exorcism

Reflections of an
Australian Catholic Exorcist

Michael Shadbolt

Published in Australia by
Coventry Press
33 Scoresby Road
Bayswater VIC 3153

ISBN 9781922589903

Copyright © Michael Shadbolt 2023

All rights reserved. Other than for the purposes and subject to the conditions prescribed under the *Copyright Act*, no part of this publication may be reproduced, stored in a retrieval system, or transmitted in any form or by any means, electronic, mechanical, photocopying, recording or otherwise, without the prior permission of the publisher.

Scripture quotations are from the *New Revised Standard Version Bible*, copyright 1989, Division of Christian Education of the National Council of the Churches of Christ in the United States of America. Used by permission. All rights reserved.

Catalogue-in-Publication entry is available from the National Library of Australia http://catalogue.nla.gov.au

Cover design by Ian James – www.jgd.com.au
Text design by Coventry Press
Set in EB Garamond

Printed in Australia

Table of Contents

Introduction	5
Background and definitions	**9**
Chapter One Background	10
Chapter Two Possession and its manifestation	16
Chapter Three The Rite of Exorcism	20
A basic modus operandi	**27**
Chapter Four Doing an exorcism	28
Chapter Five Satan's other weapons	34
Further discussion of the basic protocols	**41**
Chapter Six When not to proceed	42
Chapter Seven More on discernment	49
Chapter Eight More on 'manifestation'	61
Chapter Nine Miscellanea	67

Summaries 79

   Chapter Ten
      Security 80

   Chapter Eleven
      Dealing with a client 91

   Chapter Twelve
      Using the ritual 93

Bibliography 96

Introduction

This work is intended for priests interested in the ministry of exorcism in the Catholic Church; and for other Catholics who want to know more about this ancient ministry in the church's tradition. The book is based on my own experiences and, more importantly, on the writings of a number of priest exorcists involved in this ministry for many years. In particular, these include Fr René Chenesseau, exorcist in Paris late last century, and Fr Gabriele Amorth the famous exorcist of the diocese of Rome who died in 2016. In addition, there is Mgr Stephen J. Rossetti whose recently published work *Diary of an American Exorcist*[1] speaks eloquently of an exorcist working in an English-speaking environment.

Fr Chenesseau's book *Journal d'un Prêtre Exorciste*,[2] sadly not available in English, details his experiences mainly with priests and religious. Interspersed with these accounts is much good, no-nonsense advice on how to do exorcisms. Fr Amorth has written many books on the subject, some best sellers. The three I found most useful are his autobiography *An Exorcist Tells His Story* (1999) and two of his last works both co-authored and written

---

1 *Diary of an American Exorcist: demons, possessions, and the modern-day battle against ancient evil.* 2021. USA: Nashua, NH. Sophia Institute Press
2 *Journal d'un Prêtre Exorciste.* 2007. France: Editions Benedictines

in question and answer format, *An Exorcist Explains The Demonic* (2016), and Father Amorth, *My Battle Against Satan* (2017).

Mgr Rossetti's book[3] comprises short chapters, each dealing with or reflecting on a different aspect of the exorcist ministry. It reads like a war correspondent's reports from the front line.

Yet, if there is anything these three great priest exorcists fail to do, it is to provide us with a simple, step-by-step account of how to do an exorcism. This book seeks to offer such a 'modus operandi' – a method, a procedure, a way of working. Fr Amorth implies there should be no templates, no models. Every exorcism is different. That's undoubtedly true, but a novice in this perplexing ministry could well benefit from some guidance before entering the fray. There are things that should be avoided and others that should always be done. It helps to know these things.

Cultural factors also play an important part in the shape of possession and affect the approach needed by the exorcist. This book reflects the Australian reality with which I am familiar but I hope it is also open to the ethnic diversity of many who come seeking help.

I am indebted to my assistant, Maria (she refuses to be further identified), who has been present at the safest of the exorcisms I have performed over the last ten years. Her maturity, faith, prayer, wisdom and discretion have

---

[3] *Diary of an American Exorcist*

greatly enhanced my ministry while helping to ensure its effectiveness. I am grateful to Archbishop Hart who appointed me to this ministry some ten years ago, and to his successor Archbishop Comensoli who has allowed me to continue. Special thanks, also, to Bishop Peter Elliot for his hard work in laying the foundation of the exorcist ministry in the Melbourne Archdiocese. Above all, I thank God for his help 'in the hour of battle'.

It is my hope that my reflections and practical suggestions will be of some help to my bother priests undertaking the ministry of exorcism. There is no suggestion that this work has any official, binding authority. The only recommendation I can make is that the ideas and 'modus operandi' proposed have been widely road-tested in my ministry over the last ten years.

Background and definitions

Chapter One

Background

I have been working in the exorcism ministry for about eleven years. Archbishop Hart called me one day and gave me the Ritual for Exorcism and said, in effect, 'go for it'. I had no training or experience in exorcism before that. I made many mistakes and largely worked out a 'modus operandi' through trial and error. I would like to share with you some of the fruit of what I learned.

How important is this ministry?

Is there a real need for it, or is it just a passing fad? I can honestly say that a number of people have been significantly helped by my ministry as an exorcist over the last years. I don't want to exaggerate that number but the undoubted fruits are there. Some of these people were clearly unwell, in psychological pain and not functioning well in their lives. They were freed from something and have remained free. (Not all have kept in touch with me, but some have.) Again, I don't want to exaggerate the number of such. Of all the people I have prayed over, perhaps about 10% have had 'something' for which I felt I was helping them; indeed, it might have been less than that. I have never analysed the results of my ministry. All I know is that it has clearly helped a significant number of people.

Background

While on this point, it is important to note that exorcism is a sacramental, not a sacrament. We must not forget that our main work as priests is the celebration of Mass and the sacraments. They are the best defence against Satan. If the devil's influence over people is spreading, it's surely due in part at least to the decline in the practice of the faith. Fr Amorth, the great Italian exorcist, says that one use of the Sacrament of Confession is worth ten exorcisms. Let's keep things in perspective. You don't have to be an exorcist to be in the front line of the battle against Satan.

What qualities does an exorcist need?

You must be a person of faith, that is, the traditional faith that believes in the supernatural dimension of reality and that not everything there is good. If you haven't got this faith, you will end up just counselling people or offering advice – 'You're overtired, take time off, you need a rest', etc., etc. They will go and seek help from spiritistic charlatans who charge a fortune and use Satan's power to 'drive out Satan'. It's not going to work. We need priests of faith and also humility. In answer to the above question ('What qualities does an exorcist need?'), Fr Amorth replied – Humility, humility, humility, humility'.

You can see why. If you free someone from Satanic oppression or possession, you can feel important and special and end up as some kind of eccentric loner, doing your 'own thing'. Remember it is Jesus who drives out the evil spirits. We are only instruments in his hands. Hence, success or failure in the ministry is not ours to judge. Obedience to the bishop helps in this regard: in the Catholic Church, exorcists are appointed by the bishop.

Fr Amorth would like all priests to be able to do exorcisms by virtue of their ordination. I don't agree although, in my view, many more should be appointed than is currently the practice. Given the sensitive nature of the ministry and the risks involved, episcopal supervision is clearly advisable. In some countries, it seems, the bishop has to approve of each and every exorcism. I think that is unnecessary and likely to seriously impede the ministry. While on humility, I think it important to avoid all publicity. Media attention is more likely to do Satan's work than God's.

Do you have to be a saint?

It would undoubtedly help but you don't have to be, as is obvious. Of course, you do need to be a person of basic integrity. You're battling Satan and he will sure find any serious weaknesses. Along with humility, I would add a couple of other qualities – empathy and patience. At the same time, we should be firm when necessary. Some people seem to think that because they claim to be under attack from Satan, everyone in the church from the Pope down has to drop everything and come running.

On the question of worthiness, Mgr Rossetti writes:

> Satan will have a field day with someone who is not living priesthood with integrity. Moreover,

the exorcist should work diligently and carefully to conform his life to Christ and his Church. We exorcist priests typically go to Confession weekly, say the Divine Office with devotion, do more than one daily holy hour, and are scrupulously obedient to our superiors and to the Church. Satan will use the slightest crack in our spiritual lives to get into our heads and wreak havoc. But there is one trait above all that is essential; perhaps it is the only trait that really matters: trust. The exorcist must trust in the power of Jesus Christ, no matter how dark things may look. Jesus is Lord.[4]

Do you need to be a psychologist?

I don't think so. I have had some training at the post-graduate level in Counselling Psychology from a Melbourne-based university. While valuable and of excellent quality, the risk is that you see everything from the point of view of secular psychology and miss the spiritual. We do need to know where not to tread and when to refer people to their doctor. Some advice on this matter will be given. The ministry of Exorcism in the Catholic Church does not seek to replace or denigrate the work of psychiatrists and psychologists. We are not seeking to offer an alternative to standard medical treatment but seek only to help the small band of people who suffer from demonic attack. The 'modus operandi' recommended here suggests ways to more clearly identify the latter.

---

[4] *Diary of an American Exorcist*, p. 27.

Is it dangerous?

I asked this question of Fr José Antonio Fortea, a leading international exorcist, when he visited Melbourne some ten years ago. He replied, 'No, but you never know', or something like that. In other words, it's usually safe but there always could be an exception, much like life in general. I have never been hurt or attacked in the ministry although quite often I have been not a little frightened. Some people react under the prayer of exorcism in a way that is unsettling and threatening. (This is called 'manifestation'.)

At first, I kept a wary eye on the nearest door for a quick escape if necessary, but after a while I got used to it. Once, a lady kicked me in the shins and various clients have taken a swipe in my general direction. I felt they were held back from making contact. Should clients be restrained during exorcism? In my opinion no, but that is another issue we must deal with later when dealing with safety measures.

What about the persons you're praying over? Is it dangerous for them?

There have been reports in the media of people dying under exorcism. These were not usually under Catholic auspices although there was one infamous case in Germany in 1976 in which the young woman died and the exorcist priests were charged and convicted of murder or manslaughter (more on this later). One thing we must never do is hit or otherwise mistreat the person we are praying over. Just read the prayer. Nor should the exorcism sessions last too long.

Do we charge?

No! Also, be wary of accepting gifts. People shouldn't feel they have to give anything for our service. This is an important point that should distinguish the Catholic exorcist from the many charlatans out there who charge high prices and probably use demons to 'drive out' demons. Unlikely to work.

Chapter Two

Possession and its manifestation

It is a basic Christian belief that Satan has declared war on the Christian soul and is constantly striving to turn us away from the path that God wants us to follow. St Peter summed it up well: 'Like a roaring lion your adversary the devil prowls around, looking for someone to devour' (1 Peter 5:8). The usual weapons Satan uses in this war are temptations of one kind or another – allurements of the senses, provocation to pride, greed, lust, and the abuse of power. Let's face it; he is having no small success with this approach. Such depredations are countered by the normal, everyday ministries of the Church such as 'the word of God, the Sacraments, prayer and the fellowship of the Church'.[5] But there are other means Satan uses to attack the soul. These are called extraordinary actions of Satan, the worst of which is possession. It is rare.

Possession

Fr Amorth[6] defines possession as happening when 'a demon takes possession of a person, [and] can make him

---

5 JEREMY DAVIES. *Exorcism: Understanding Exorcism in Scripture and Practice.* 2009. London: Catholic Truth Society, p. 26.
6 *An Exorcist Explains the Demonic.* 2016. USA: Manchester, NH: Sophia Institute Press, p. 66.

say and do what he wishes. It is necessary to clarify that the devil is not able to take possession of the soul of a man (unless the person expressly consents to it), but only his body'. Fr Tanquerey writes 'Two elements constitute possession: the presence of the demon in the body of the possessed and the dominion exercised by the demon over that body and, through it, over the soul'.[7]

Fr Poulain, classic spiritual writer of early last century, wrote that with possession although 'the place is captured... the citadel itself, where the higher faculties, the intelligence, and the will are to be found' remain free.[8] Hence, since the higher faculties remain intact, it is not a mental sickness although the longer the situation lasts the more likely is such an outcome. I like to compare it with a house invader who breaks in and decides to stay, becoming more dominant and controlling as time passes. The householder would become increasingly more oppressed and miserable. In my years as an exorcist, I have seen that look of desperation in the eyes of the possessed and have rejoiced to see it gradually lift as the exorcism proceeds. I have also noted that the longer the evil spirit has been there, the longer it takes to shift it.

The Problem

The Rite of Exorcism is the means the Church has at its disposal to free a person possessed by an evil spirit.

---

[7] Quoted in Davies *Exorcism*, p. 28.
[8] AUGUSTINE POULAIN SJ. *The Graces of Interior Prayer: a treatise on mystical theology*. 1978. USA. Westminster, VT: Celtic Cross Books, p. 428.

The problem is that not all who claim to be possessed or fear they might be are, in fact, so afflicted. Earlier centuries, the seventeenth and eighteenth especially, saw an epidemic of such claims leading to truly scandalous scenes.[9] The publication of the 1614 Ritual was meant to put a damper on such excesses. The exorcist should treat all claims of demonic infestation with a degree of scepticism, put all such claims to the test. The problem is, what test?

Manifestation

'Manifestation' is the term used to describe the most remarkable phenomenon associated with exorcisms. It refers to the sudden onset of unusual behaviour in the person being prayed over. It might be shaking all over, gesticulating angrily, yelling out, snarling, hissing, falling on the floor, vomiting or dry retching, crying, going stiff as a board, fainting, stomping around the room or the adoption of weird postures. In some cases, the reaction can be severe and frightening; in others, it is mild and barely noticeable such as a grimacing of the face or a turning up of the eyes. Sometimes the person falls asleep. Occasionally, the demon comes out with mocking laughter or half-choked utterances such as 'I'm not going'. I have never seen anyone levitating or heard foreign languages but a common feature is a look of sheer hatred on the face of the one being exorcised.

---

9 See JEAN LHERMITE. *True or False Possession?: how to distinguish the demonic from the demented*. 2013. USA: Manchester, NH: Sophia Institute Press.

Some authors claim the person becomes unconscious during manifestation. I haven't seen that often, but it may be that such persons are not so much unconscious as not fully aware of what they are doing in this state. For the exorcist, however, it doesn't really matter. You just keep on praying the Rite until the session is finished.

The understanding is that these reactions are the evil spirit manifesting its presence. They can be frightening at times, but with experience you get used to it and just keep on praying. Because of the noise sometimes involved, it might be a good idea not to do exorcisms in the church but in a less frequented part of the parish hall or offices. Otherwise, you might have the police turning up.

Conclusion

It is my contention that 'manifestation' as described here is the strongest indication of the presence of an evil spirit in a person being prayed over. It is not certain by any means and hence requires further testing. But if a person manifests during an initial exorcism, you invite that person to return for further sessions – the process of exorcism begins. It is worth noting that it is what happens during the recitation of the Rite that matters. People might report some or all of the above mentioned phenomena occurring in the life of the person. If it doesn't happen during the recitation of the Rite, it is not taken as such a strong sign of possession.

Chapter Three

The Rite of Exorcism

An exorcism is performed by reading the Rite of Exorcism over persons thought to be possessed by evil spirits. The Rite is the principal instrument used to effect an exorcism. Its prayers and formulae should not be altered.

The old and the new

The Rite was first published by the Church in 1614 with the title *De Exorcisandis Obsessis a Daemonio*. A revised version was published in 1998 under Pope St John Paul II – *De Exorcismis Et Supplicationibus Quibusdam*. The new rite is essentially the same as the old, perhaps a little shorter. The most notable difference is that in the new version a distinction is more clearly drawn between the prayers asking God's help in delivering the affected person and those commanding the demon to depart. The former is listed under the heading of *Formula deprecativa*, the latter under *Formula imperativa*. I found the latter to be the more powerful and are clearly what exorcism is all about.

Addressing Satan

Another significant difference is that the new version omits a command addressed to the demon to reveal its name and the date and hour of its departure (Paragraph 2, p. 329 of the old version). It makes sense. Given that Satan is 'a liar and the father of lies' (John 8:44), it would be foolish to believe anything he said. Moreover, there is a danger that, in addressing the demon in this way, the exorcist is encouraged to enter into some sort of dialogue with the evil spirit. This should never be done. Just keep reading the prayers of the Rite regardless of whether the evil spirit mocks you, insults you or tries to argue with you.

Which rite?

According to Fr Amorth, a priest is allowed to use either the old ritual or the new. I use a mixture of both, having obtained an English translation of the old ritual which I use for its litanies and Bible readings as well as a number of its prayers commanding Satan to leave. Then, with the new ritual in Latin, I pray one 'deprecativa' prayer and two or three of the 'imperativa' prayers. This way, an exorcism lasts about half an hour.

Some people ask for the old rite alone in Latin. I usually oblige although I haven't found it any stronger than the new rite in Latin. I personally like the idea of a mixture of English and Latin; if the new rite has an English translation (I have heard that one is in preparation), I would read the opening prayers, litanies and Bible readings in English then a mixture of one 'deprecativa' and two or more 'imperativa' prayers also in English. After that, I would repeat the 'imperativa' prayers in Latin. Mgr Rossetti says that 'the 1614 Rite of Exorcism in Latin remains the general favourite of exorcists'.[10]

How much time does an exorcism take?

Jesus exorcised people with just a word in a minute or two. With us, or at least with me, it is not so simple or so quick. Fr Amorth writes that he prayed over some people for weeks, months and, in some cases, years. Obviously, he was talking about an exorcism being spread out over many sessions. This squares with my experience. Most successful exorcisms I have been involved in took up to six months – of one session a week – and there have been two or three that lasted over years, eventually with success – the people were completely liberated.

So, you can see that the ministry of exorcism requires some commitment. Imagine reading the same prayer over the same person once a week for a couple of years. I have found that exorcism is a process spread out over many sessions lasting, in all, weeks or months and sometimes longer. (How do you know when to stop? That also is something we'll deal with later.)

---

10 *Diary of an American Exorcist*, p. 106.

Perhaps a more important question is how long does a session last?

Reading the Rite over a person takes about twenty minutes. Of course, the exorcist may repeat any or all of the prayers as often as he deems fit. In my opinion, a session should never last longer than an hour at the most, and as a rule last only twenty minutes to half an hour. You can't go on much longer than that; as a busy priest, you haven't the time or the energy, and, more importantly, sessions lasting hours risk the wellbeing of the person being prayed over. After half an hour, you call a halt to the proceedings, no matter how shaken up the person might be. You do so gently but firmly, allowing them time to recover, and invite them back – same time, same place – next week. The effect of the prayer usually carries over. That, at least, has been my experience and I recommend it. It is an important safety measure.

Implements used?

Apart from the ritual itself, the exorcist carries a blessed crucifix and some holy water. He is dressed in an alb and stole. The stole can be placed around the shoulders of the person being prayed over at a couple of points in the ceremony. Likewise, hands may be laid on the head or shoulders of the client in a gesture of imparting the Holy Spirit. Apart from that, you don't touch the person at all. You just read the Rite in a calm and authoritative voice. You may raise the voice at times but that's all.

Should the demon speak, the exorcist never responds but keeps on praying. There must be no attempt to hasten the evil spirit's departure by hitting or otherwise abusing the person. Jesus is the one who does the exorcism and the exorcist is only an instrument in his hands.

Whereabouts?

Most authorities recommend that an exorcism be done in the church. I found the priest's office to be better suited. It's better to be on a day or hour when the secretary or other parish workers are absent. The noise that sometimes occurs can be frightening.

An assistant

You should never do an exorcism alone. Ideally, the preference would be to have a group of people assisting – three or four praying, a psychologist, and perhaps one or two others to help with any unexpected disturbances. In practice, in an Australian parish setting, it's going to be difficult to organise such a gathering on a regular basis. But you should have an assistant at all times, preferably a woman of mature years and faith. She should leave during the initial interview but otherwise be present at all times.

The assistant must never say any of the prayers of exorcism but pray in a general way for a successful outcome. She may de-brief with the exorcist afterwards and alert him to aspects of the case he may have missed. Of course, both the exorcist and the assistant must observe professional secrecy, never divulging to others things that have happened during an exorcism. If dealing with a teenager, it is important to have a parent or guardian present as well as the assistant. Likewise, with a child, although I have never exorcised a child and would be very reluctant to do so unless a child psychologist were also involved.

Types of Exorcism

Exorcism can be **major** or **minor**. Major is what we are talking about. It involves use of the Ritual of Exorcism and can be done only by an officially appointed priest. Minor exorcism comprises prayers of simple deliverance which anyone can say.

Major exorcism can also be **liturgical** or **private**. The liturgical is done in church with some if not all of the liturgical trappings. I have never done this and don't think I ever would. It seems to me an affront to the privacy of the person being prayed over. If the person asked for this, you would have to wonder if there were not some exhibitionism involved. Some people seem to get an ego boost from the idea that Satan has singled them out for special attention. The genuinely possessed would not think this way.

An exorcism can also be *exploratory*. Both Amorth and Chenesseau say that the surest way of discerning whether an exorcism is needed is by doing an exorcism. Amorth[11] speaks of such as 'the best diagnostic instrument', and Chenesseau[12] compares it to a surgeon who does exploratory surgery to see if a further operation is needed. I call exorcisms of this kind 'exploratory'. (I am not sure if anyone else uses this term.) Most exorcisms I do are of this type. If an exploratory exorcism gives signs of demonic possession, then this justifies a definitive exorcism in which the same Ritual prayer is repeated over multiple subsequent sessions.

Scriptural basis

There are many texts from the Gospels that show Jesus did many exorcisms. Adam C. Blai[13] has a comprehensive list of the relevant Bible passages. There is one incident from the Gospels that I have found encouraging. On this occasion, the disciples asked Jesus why they had been unable to cast out an evil spirit from a boy. Jesus replied that 'This kind can come out only by prayer and fasting' (Mark 9:28-29). This implies that an exorcism can take a long time. Most of the exorcism I have been involved in required many sessions in which the prayer of exorcism (the Rite) was repeated over many weeks or months or even longer in some cases before deliverance was achieved. I identify with those unnamed disciples.

---

11 *An Exorcist Explains the Demonic*, p. 99.
12 *Journal d'un Prêtre Exorciste*, p. 12.
13 *Hauntings, possessions and exorcisms*. 2017. USA: Steubenville, OH: Emmaus Road Publishing, pp. 109-120.

A basic modus operandi

Chapter Four

Doing an exorcism

Following Fr Chenesseau,[14] there are three parts or stages in doing an exorcism. Different terms could be used for these stages, but they refer to the same thing: 1) The initial interview, then, if the decision is taken to proceed, 2) Reading the Rite, and 3) Observing the effects if any and acting accordingly. All three stages play a part in the process of discerning whether or not the person has an evil spirt. Both Chenesseau and Amorth stress that mild scepticism is the preferred attitude of the Catholic exorcist throughout the process. Indeed, Chenesseau implies that the only way of knowing for sure that a person has an evil spirit is if that person gets better at the end of the process.

    1. The initial interview. The exorcist meets with the person seeking help. Apart from asking the name of the person and a few other personal details, the main purpose is to detect any signs or symptoms of diabolic activity in the life of the person. Such evidence comes in answer to the questions – 'What is happening in your life?' or 'Why do you think you need an exorcism?' The reports given should never be taken as certain evidence of diabolical possession even if they describe extraordinary

---

14 *Journal d'un Prêtre Exorciste.*

behaviours. Some people have great imaginations. At best, the signs and symptoms can only indicate the possibility of diabolic involvement.

Another important purpose of the initial interview is to see if there are reasons for **not** proceeding with an exorcism. In general, such reasons would be serious mental health issues and religious or spiritual beliefs significantly at variance with mainstream Christianity. Such might be, for example, deep involvement in occult practices and belief in reincarnation. Of course, if the person has serious intent to get away from these beliefs and practices, then you might consider continuing with the next stage. (How to manage the initial interview – especially regarding mental health issues – is further dealt with in chapter 6.)

2. Reading the Rite. If there is no serious reason against doing an exorcism and some indication that diabolic activity might be present, then the exorcist proceeds to the next stage and performs an exorcism by praying the Rite over the person. As I have said, I call this first exorcism 'an exploratory exorcism' since its main purpose is to further discern the presence or otherwise of an evil spirit. Once again, the exploratory exorcism offers no certainty that a person is possessed, but it is a stronger indication than that provided by the initial interview. The Rite of Exorcism is read over the person and the reaction is carefully noted. In my opinion, this is the critical stage in the exorcism process.

3. **Observing the effects.** Depending on what happens during the exploratory exorcism, the following decisions are taken. There are three possible outcomes.
A. *Nothing happens.* The person does not react in any way during the reading of the Rite. There is no manifestation. This is by far the most common outcome. The person is advised that they are not possessed by an evil spirit and no further sessions are arranged. Some clients object to this outcome, insisting that they are possessed. You could arrange for a couple more sessions, praying the Rite over them again. Any more than that would be ill advised. Some people, although not possessed, are clearly in need of further prayer, prayers of healing for example, or prayers of support. But is it the role of the exorcist, working as exorcist, to provide this type of prayer? At best, your appointment book will fill up; at worst, you could encourage delusional thinking in some clients.

(There are two situations when you might use Rite of Exorcism over people who don't manifest. These are cases of Satanic oppression and vexation. In neither case do sufferers manifest, but they are under Satanic attack. These situations are dealt with in the next chapter.)
B. *The person manifests.* It can be light, extremely violent or somewhere in between. When this happens, the client is invited to return 'same time next week', or sooner if the exorcist thinks it fit. At this point, the exorcism as such begins. It may take many subsequent

sessions lasting weeks, months or in some cases years. The exorcist should expect to see a gradual lessening or weakening in the strength of the manifestations as the sessions proceed, although they may worsen over the initial sessions. It is important to note that the attenuation can be very slow in coming but across a few sessions (say up to eight or ten) it should be evident. Eventually, the manifestations all but disappear. The clients will declare they are better or simply not turn up any more. Chenesseau[15] also speaks of the person beginning to look better, freer and happier after a session or two. This is true, but I prefer to rely more on the weakening of the manifestations no matter how gradual. The former could be due to the placebo effect.

C. *The person manifests but there is no change.* After a couple of months, perhaps eight or ten sessions, there is no indication of any weakening in the manifestation. In this case, the exorcism should be brought to a close and the process stopped. Something else is happening. What? Some possibilities are: a) the evil spirit is too strong for us. Chenesseau[16] says this can happen. You can't win them all. b) the person may be suffering from a mental health issue which is the underlying problem. Satan hides behind it. c) the person may be manufacturing or feigning the manifestation. We have all read the books, seen

---
15 *Journal d'un Prêtre Exorciste*
16 Ibid.

the films. With experience, the exorcist can pick this up but the major give-away is that, over subsequent sessions, there is no attenuation in the manifestations shown. In my early days, when I lacked experience, one client was still manifesting fiercely twelve months later. What the problem was I don't know, but I should have picked it up much sooner. That exorcism was going nowhere.

Summary

According to the 'modus operandi' advocated here, the exploratory exorcism is the critical stage in the exorcism process. You first do an exploratory exorcism and then, if the person manifests, repeat the prayer in subsequent sessions until the manifestation fades away. If the client does not manifest, you conclude it's not possession. Likewise, if there is manifestation but no eventual attenuation across subsequent sessions, you also conclude it is not possession.

Objection: If the exploratory exorcism is the critical stage, why bother with the initial interview?

You should always do an initial interview. It is important to know something about the person and more important to know if there is any reason for not proceeding with an exorcism, such as a serious mental health issue. Also, there should be some sign or symptoms from the life of the person indicating that possession by a demon could be involved. This is not easily ascertained but if it's a possibility I usually proceed with an exploratory exorcism. (This issue is dealt with again in chapter seven mainly under '**Signs and Symptoms**'.)

Objection: Discernment of an evil spirit presence is the critical work of the exorcist. It should be done and dusted before beginning to pray the Rite over a person.

Both Fr Chenesseau and Fr Amorth say that actually doing an exorcism – praying the Rite over clients – is the surest way of knowing if they are possessed. This concurs with my experience. Not infrequently, I have interviewed people who showed no clear signs of diabolical possession. But when I prayed the Rite over them by way of exploration, they suddenly burst forth in manifestation. That's why I think it a mistake to hand over the work of discernment *in toto* to others during the exorcism process. (This issue is touched on again in chapter nine.)

Chapter Five

Satan's other weapons

Possession is regarded as an extraordinary means of Satanic attack for which exorcism is the principal counter weapon. But, it is generally agreed that, apart from *possession*, there are other extraordinary forms of Satanic attack for which special prayers may be helpful. These forms are *oppression* (or *obsession*), *vexation*, and *infestation*. The prayers indicated are prayers of simple deliverance which both priests and lay people can pray over others without permission from the bishop. However, it's my opinion that an exorcist priest (and only he) could pray the Rite of Exorcism in these cases in certain circumstances. The Rite of Exorcism is a powerful prayer which I believe should be made available to people who, although not possessed, are under heavy attack from Satan.

The problem is that those suffering *oppression*, *obsession*, and *vexation* do not manifest under the prayer. Hence, there is lacking that clear sign of Satanic involvement and any chance, therefore, of observing a loosening of the demon's grip over subsequent sessions.

OPPRESSION

Oppression is a sharply focused and concerted attack on an individual by Satan attacking from without. It could be compared to a city under siege. It is something more than a mere temptation but not *possession*. 'People suffering from demonic oppression are generally in great distress... They often have secondary health and mental problems. They may despair of help and feel that God has abandoned them'.[17] It is clear that mental health issues may be to the fore in demonic oppression and may be the principal problem. For that reason, it is probably advisable to leave cases of claimed *oppression* to others praying prayers of simple deliverance.

In tragic circumstances

There is one oppressive situation, however, in which the Rite of Exorcism could help people. It occurs when the principal cause of the *oppression* being experienced comes from an external life event of tragic nature, such as the death of a loved one, the loss of something precious, or a crisis in a person's marriage or priestly vocation. It could also be used, I believe, in cases of post-abortion trauma and where there has been involvement in false religion or occult practices. Internal psychological and emotional distress are present in all such cases, but the main precipitating cause is an outside or exogenous (external) life event.

I have used the Rite of Exorcism in these circumstances, repeating it at intervals through the height of the crisis.

---

17 BLAI, *Hauntings, possessions and exorcisms*, pp. 54-55.

No doubt Satan attacks at times like this. If used in this way, the Rite should only be used through the worst of the crisis. It should not become part of on-going prayer support. I have found that people are helped by the prayer of exorcism in these circumstances especially when feeling close to despair.

The Rite should not be used in this way if the main cause of the *oppression* is bodily sickness since we have the Sacrament of the Sick for that. A sacrament is far stronger than any sacramental. Nor should it be used if the main cause of the crisis is an internal mental health issue. Where the precipitating cause is a serious mental health issue, leave all such cases to the medical profession.

OBSESSION

Some authors list 'obsession' as another extraordinary means of Satanic attack.[18] Most often, this refers to obsessive or intrusive thoughts and since these are usually an internal, mental health phenomenon, they are best left to psychologists for treatment. However, there is one such situation, fortunately rare, where the Rite of Exorcism could be used by an exorcist priest. It is when a good, practising Christian has their prayer life constantly invaded by ugly, blasphemous thoughts. Sufferers are extremely distressed. I have prayed the Rite over such people, repeating it until the situation improved. The

---

[18] E.g. AMORTH, *An Exorcist Tells his Story*, p. 34.

person may need a 'booster' session every so often. If there is no change, refer the person to a psychologist.

VEXATION

Vexation is a strange phenomenon and one that, at first sight, certainly looks like a mental health issue. The term is used for paranormal happenings directed against the individual often – but not exclusively – at night. It involves unexplained sounds, lights going on or off by themselves, doors opening or closing, shapes and shadows, threatening miasmas (unpleasant atmospheres) in the air, marks appearing on the body, and someone or something grabbing an arm or leg in bed at night. It all sounds like hallucination and we must be alert to the possibility of mental health issues (especially if the emphasis is on hearing voices). Clients of this kind usually present with much distress especially fear, their lives becoming increasingly disrupted. They also tend to be embarrassed by it all. They need our help.

Psychologist and auxiliary member of the International Association of Exorcists in Rome, Adam C. Blai rejects the idea of praying for people who claim paranormal experiences. He writes: 'Over a short time, it became clear to me that most people with paranormal complaints are just having false experiences due to sleep disorders mental or medical illness, medication effects, or aging'.[19]

---

19 *Hauntings, possessions and exorcisms*, p. 93.

It has been my experience, however, that people complaining of the paranormal events described above have responded well when the Rite of Exorcism has been prayed over them. I think its use should be considered.

Don't treat for 'vexation' if the person seeking help has been deeply involved in occult practices. (See the section in chapter nine on 'witchcraft and the occult'.)

Great improvement

People suffering from *vexation* never manifest under the prayer of exorcism. Many, however, show improvement after just one session. Usually, only a few sessions are needed although some may require more and some a 'booster' prayer every now and then. I usually let them decide if they need more prayer. Obviously, if they don't show any improvement after several sessions you would suggest they see a psychologist. If you find them expanding the illusion – saying things such as 'Oh, it's really the neighbours next door' or 'I think the police are behind it' – you rebuke them for paying attention to Satan's mind games.

Our understanding of vexation is that it is nothing but Satan playing tricks on the mind. Not only do the exorcism prayers help drive Satan away, they also embolden the sufferer to confront and resist Satan's tricks. But if you find the client is not improving and repeatedly returning for further prayer, it would be better to refer them to a doctor. Likewise, if the sufferer is a child presented by a parent it is better to refer them both to a child psychologist. There may be something in the parent-child relationship that is pathological. (Sometimes, however, the child is not the problem. The parent is too embarrassed to admit to the condition. If you suspect this is happening, pray the Rite over both at once with focus on the parent. It will soon become clear who the sufferer is.)

It is stressed that only an authorised priest exorcist is permitted to use the Rite of Exorcism in these circumstances. Others may pray against *vexation*, and also *oppression*, using prayers of deliverance but not exorcism. Overall, I have found these prayers, especially against vexation, to have been very helpful to the sufferers concerned.

INFESTATION

Infestation refers to haunted houses and the like. The problem here is that it involves travelling and makes one feel like a 'ghost buster'. But I have prayed against evil spirits in a few houses usually close to my parish, going from room to room and throwing much holy water around while praying prayers from the Rite. I have never felt or seen anything on these occasions. Some of the residents reported that things were better subsequently. As a rule, I tend to think that it is the people who need praying over, not their dwellings.

Conclusion

The Rite of Exorcism is meant for people suffering from *possession*. There are three other circumstances, however, when an authorised priest exorcist could pray prayers from the Rite of Exorcism. One would be in cases of *oppression*, that is, at times of crisis precipitated by an external, exogenous life event or occult involvement. The other circumstances where the Rite could be used are in cases of *obsession* and *vexation* as defined above. In all three circumstances, the exorcism prayers should not become part of on-going prayer support, although an occasional 'booster' session might be in order.

(I have also used the Rite of Exorcism over people who have been harmed by serious involvement in the occult. They may have opened themselves up to Satan. As indicated above, there is a section on this in chapter nine.)

Further discussion of the basic protocols

Chapter Six

When not to proceed

An exorcist should always want to help people but there are cases when it is better not to proceed with an exorcism even if he thinks the client 'might have something'. The main reasons are serious mental health issues and religious and spiritual beliefs at variance with Christianity. These problems are best picked up during the initial interview or even the first contact over the phone or internet.

The initial interview should be brief; it's not an interrogation. Apart from the general questions – 'What has brought you here?' or 'Why do you need an exorcism?', there needs be a question such as –'How is your health, especially mental or emotional health?' You may need to ask, 'Have you ever had a mental health diagnosis? Are you on medication?' You might also include questions about involvement in New Age practices such as Reiki.

Whatever the answer, I usually do an exploratory exorcism then and there, shortening the prayers a little. In my experience, people with mental health issues do not manifest. For that reason, the Rite is not repeated and the exorcism process terminated. No harm, I believe, is done to sufferers if there is just one session. Advice would usually be given that, since the cause of their problem is not spiritual, they see a doctor or psychologist.

However, there are some circumstances regarding mental health when it is better not to get involved at all, or to proceed with caution. Here are situations which I have encountered. There may be others.

MENTAL HEALTH REASONS

1. Someone presents complaining of demonic attack in a rather agitated, panicky or desperate way. This usually happens at the first contact over the phone, and very often it is another person speaking for the sufferer. They ask for immediate help and speak as if a demonic attack were actually in progress. The only response in this circumstance is to advise them to call a doctor quickly or, better, get the sufferer to Emergency at the nearest hospital. They may be having a breakdown or be on the verge of a psychotic episode, often drug induced.
2. Never pray the Rite of Exorcism over anyone who is about to enter hospital, just out of hospital or still under the frequent, regular care of psychiatrists. If asked, you would pray only supportive prayer along with the sacraments. Under no circumstance would a Catholic exorcist pray the Rite in a hospital or clinical setting. Sometimes people under regular psychiatric care plead for exorcism. Tell them to get a letter from their doctor agreeing to this. You need to make sure

the doctor knows they want exorcism and not just Hail Marys and prayers of support.

3. Not infrequently, people ask for exorcism presenting a lengthy, strange, rather incoherent story. It doesn't quite hang together in a meaningful narrative. It may also contain bizarre descriptions of demons seen or messages heard. Often, the story comes in an e-mail they send along with the request for exorcism. The possibility of serious mental health issues in such cases is clear. At times, in these cases, I have asked for a report from the person's doctor before proceeding. It is rarely forthcoming. At other times, I have excused myself saying the case is far too complex for me, way above my pay grade, beyond my knowledge and experience.

In my experience, people genuinely infected with an evil spirit say little in the initial interview. They just look miserable, despondent and, if anything, embarrassed. They're the ones more likely to 'manifest' when subjected to an exploratory exorcism. By contrast, people who have written a couple of pages on their condition seldom react under the prayers of exorcism.

4. Sadly, there are some who don't answer truthfully to the question about mental health issues in the past − 'No, Father, it's not that, I'm sure', they reply. It might be true but often it's not. In this case you have little option but to do an exploratory exorcism over them. Two things can happen: a) *they manifest*. In that case, you then arrange for subsequent sessions, expecting to see some attenuation in the strength of

the manifestation, albeit very slight, as time goes on. Or b) *they don't manifest*. In that case, you leave it at that. Some of these may insist that you continue to pray the Rite over them in further sessions, claiming that 'many spirits left during the prayer today'. You have to be gentle but firm in these cases. It's possible these clients have serious mental health issues which they won't face.

> Mental disorders of most concern to an exorcist would be those involving delusional thinking. Such would include, psychosis, delusional ideation (e.g. 'I'm Jesus Christ'), and schizophrenia. The last mentioned is probably the most challenging since sufferers can interpret their 'voices' as demonic. Moreover, the condition is often not apparent to non-professionals in mental health. There is more on this condition in chapter 9. PTSD may also be of concern.

5. In a very few cases, in my experience, parents have presented an adolescent for exorcism who had special developmental needs such as autism. Don't get involved in these cases; explain to the parents that this is a medical not a spiritual issue.

    More common are elderly folk who start seeing things in the night. I usually pray the Rite over them but never with any effect. They ring back saying, 'The prayer was nice, but it didn't work'. It's probably cognitive decline although I wonder if some holy old people might be receiving intimations of the next world, a sort of early near-death experience. Little wonder an exorcism doesn't work.

More common still are people who ask for exorcism for an elderly parent or relative who has become uncharacteristically nasty and aggressive. It's most likely Alzheimer's although you could do an exploratory exorcism to prove it isn't spiritual.

6. Rarer but more concerning are cases in which people ask for exorcism against evil spirits they claim are pressuring them to suicide or to a criminal act against others. Don't attempt to deal with these cases. They need to see a doctor or psychologist for help with obsessive or intrusive thoughts.

7. I have never prayed the Rite of Exorcism over a child and would be very wary of so doing. If asked, I pray prayers of simple deliverance. If people insist that more is needed, you should consult with the bishop first or more experienced exorcists. The main protagonist in the film *The Exorcist* was a child, but that film is not to be taken seriously as a guide.

I have prayed over some teenagers with very good outcomes. You must make sure that a parent or guardian is present during all sessions of the exorcism. It is also necessary to make sure the teenager wants the prayer. Briefly talk to them alone if necessary.

RELIGIOUS REASONS

1. Some people – while rational and coherent – are into strange religions involving such things as astral travel, reincarnation, and other occult concepts. One man, describing himself as 'a practitioner of the paranormal', asked me to exorcise two ventriloquist dolls, another informed me he had been reincarnated at age twelve. I excused myself, saying I operated only within the doctrinal parameters of the Catholic Church. (It is different if the person wants to leave such involvement and fears they have been contaminated by it.)
2. Some Catholic authors say we should only exorcise practising Catholics. I have never insisted on that requirement and have prayed for non-Catholics, non-Christians and even unbelievers as long as they expressed no advocacy of beliefs hostile to the Christian Faith and came genuinely seeking help. (Jesus exorcised pagans.) Whether this is the best approach is up to the exorcist to decide since there is no official teaching from the Church on this matter. Of course, I always suggest to clients that they get their lives in right order and seek God. With Christians, especially Catholics, I urge them to return to the practice of the Faith. Some have.
3. Others keep asking that you pray the Rite over them at regular intervals, every few months or so. These are clients who did not manifest during the exploratory exorcism, thereby showing no evidence of possession.

The Rite of Exorcism is not meant to be used as an on-going supportive prayer.
4. Some people ask for exorcism who are seriously involved in the New Age or occult practices. Don't comply unless they show a willingness to abandon the occult and give their heart completely to Jesus Christ. I suspect that some of these people see exorcism as just another magic formula in the occult arsenal.

Chapter Seven

More on discernment

To do an exorcism you must have some evidence that the client is possessed or has an evil spirit. Discernment is the process by which you decide if there is such evidence. This is at the heart of the exorcism ministry and the most difficult aspect. The exorcism itself is easy. You simply read the Rite over the clients. The problem is in determining whether they need an exorcism in the first place and, if they do, how many times do you repeat the prayer over them.

Self-diagnosis

One thing is certain – you can't rely on a person's claim to be possessed. In my early days as an exorcist I prayed the Rite over just about everyone who fronted up. If they said it was helping them, I continued to do so through subsequent sessions. One client from those days would say at the end of every session 'two spirits left today', 'six this week', 'many more today' and so on. Two years later it was still 'six left today', or whatever. Eventually, there was a break down. The psychiatrist, so I heard, told him to 'keep away from those exorcists'. The lesson is clear. You can't rely on a person's self-diagnosis. It is evident that some people would much rather believe the devil is possessing them than admit they have a mental health problem.

How do you discern the presence of an evil spirit in a person? What are the signs of possession? Sadly, it's not so straightforward. There are at least four approaches to the problem – 'signs and symptoms', 'the classic approach', 'the psychological approach', and that of 'the exploratory exorcism'.

SIGNS AND SYMPTOMS

The 'signs and symptoms' approach looks for indications of demonic influence in the life of people, in their thoughts, desires, feelings and behaviours. Chenesseau[20] deals at length with this approach dividing the signs into those indicating loss of inner peace and joy, those indicating the absence of faith, hope and charity, often expressed in hatred of God and holy things, and, thirdly, persistent health problems of both a psychiatric and physical nature that can't be explained. Information of this kind usually comes mainly during the first meeting with the invitation to 'tell me what's happening in your life'.

Critique of the 'signs and symptoms'

These signs and symptoms may well indicate the possibility of possession but they offer no certain proof, a fact that

---

20 *Journal d'un Prêtre Exorciste*, pp. 146-240.

Chenesseau acknowledges. They need something else to be more certain.

THE CLASSIC APPROACH

The 1614 ritual listed the following as signs of possession by an evil spirit: 'uttering long sentences [not learnt by heart] in an unknown tongue, or understanding those who speak this language, revealing future or hidden things [especially having a clear knowledge of the future or of various sciences], displaying powers beyond one's age, condition, and other similar things; *when several of these signs are combined,* the indications are *more conclusive*'.[21]

To this list of preternatural signs, Fr. Amorth (2016) adds: 'the person exorcised can spit nails, glass, or hair. These objects... materialize in the vomit coming out of the mouth'.[22] Adam C. Blai adds yet another 'levitation... when the body rises off the floor and floats six to ten inches off the ground'.[23]

The new ritual, published by the Vatican in 1998 (Section III, *Praenotanda,* para. 16) repeats the three classic

---

21 Quoted in POULAIN, *The Graces of Interior Prayer,* p. 433. Italics in original.
22 *An Exorcist Explains the Demonic,* p. 104. There is a condition known as Morgellons syndrome, symptoms of which are fibrous substances forming on or in the body, often in various shapes. It is on the psychiatric spectrum but others attribute it to parasites. Few blame Satan.
23 *Hauntings, Possessions and Exorcisms,* p. 60.

signs of possession and adds some other signs of a moral and spiritual nature: 'a vehement aversion to God, to the Holy Name of Jesus, to the Blessed Virgin Mary and the Saints, to the Church, to the word of God, to holy things, to rites especially sacramentals and to sacred images'. This addition means the Church recognises there may be other signs of demonic presence beside the long-standing classic indicators.

Critique of the classic approach

Reliance on the classic or preternatural signs in discerning the need for exorcism has largely disappeared in modern times. Fr Poulain, writing originally in 1910, questioned the validity of these signs: 'The ritual... does not state that the above signs always give a complete certainty, especially if they occur separately'.[24] The sign of 'abnormal strength' could be 'purely of the natural order' and 'knowledge of distant things' could be due to 'supra-normal states... which [are] not supernatural.'[25]

While in one of his last books,[26] Fr Amorth seems to endorse the preternatural signs as necessary for the discernment of an evil spirit presence, in his earlier and major work, it is evident he did not rely on the preternatural signs in his own work as an exorcist. He called for care and a degree of scepticism about such

---

24 *The Graces of Interior Prayer*, p. 434.
25 Ibid.
26 *My Battle against Satan*, p. 76.

things while, at the same time, warning against having a closed mind; balance is needed.

He writes: 'We believe that indirectly the Ritual ... warn[s] the exorcist not to be too quick to detect a satanic presence. The Ritual then sets out other norms warning the exorcist against the many tricks that Satan uses to disguise his presence. We exorcists believe it is right to guard against being fooled by those who are psychologically ill, or not subject to any demonic influence, and therefore do not need us in any way. However, there is also the opposite danger – and today it is much more frequent and therefore more to be feared – the danger of not recognising an evil presence and of denying an exorcism when it is requested. An unnecessary exorcism never harmed anyone. All the exorcists whom I questioned agree with me'.[27]

One thing is clear: few exorcists today would see the classic signs as a *sine qua non* of doing an exorcism. Even if present, you should still maintain a degree of scepticism. In my own experience – for what it is worth – I have never clearly encountered any of the supernatural or preternatural signs listed in the old or new Ritual. Once, a teenage girl, 18 or 19 years, was brought in and restrained by her dad and an uncle, two burly blokes, who seemed barely able to hold her while I recited the Rite of Exorcism over her. Even so, I doubt it was herculean strength beyond her years.

---

27 *An Exorcist Tells his Story*. p. 45.

I suspect that the almost total disappearance of the ministry of exorcism in the Church since the 18th century has been due to the insistence on supernatural signs before beginning an exorcism. Fr Amorth hints at this possibility.[28] The only miraculous thing I've seen as an exorcist is the marvellous liberation some people have experienced through this ministry. Others have been helped by it. The nonsense associated with this ministry can be extreme and picking your way through that is not easy. But fruits there are.

THE PSYCHOLOGICAL APPROACH

This approach uses psychology to sift out unsuitable candidates for exorcism. Those with identifiable psychopathology are rejected. Mgr Rossetti, famous US priest author and exorcist, describes how he discerns the need for an exorcism:

> 'A middle-aged woman complained that she was possessed by demons that were put into her by public officials but she couldn't complain because they're 'in' on it. Paranoid. Again, no.
> Then I received an email, full of loose associations and bizarre reasoning claiming possession by a demon. Major thought disorder. No.
> But then one caught my eye. The person sounded fairly sane. She had a long list of unexplained illnesses. She tried many doctors and none of them

---

28 *An Exorcist Explains the Demonic*, p. 99.

knew what was wrong. She had recently come back to the practice of the faith. Previously she had been involved in the occult but eventually realized her mistake. Now when she tries to receive communion she gets ill. She finds it increasingly difficult even to walk to church. Hmmm. Maybe.

This last one bears a closer look: a possible case of oppression, perhaps even possession. We will ask for much background information, subject the person to a psychologist's eye, and then set up an appointment, to include praying over her. We will note how she reacts to the prayers. We shall see.'[29]

Critique of the psychological approach

This approach certainly identifies those with serious mental health issues. As indicated in the previous chapter, it is better not to proceed with an exorcism in these cases. However, there are a number of problems with this approach:

- It tends to medicalise the exorcism process. It makes a psychological diagnosis the arbiter.
- For this approach to work, you need to have a trained psychologist on the team. In a normal Australian parish setting that's something that can't be guaranteed on a regular basis.
- One solution would be to insist that prospective candidates for exorcism visit a psychologist before

---

[29] *Diary of an American Exorcist*, pp. 37-38.

beginning the exorcism process. If you do this, very few people will return for the exorcism. They have come for prayer and are likely to be put off by an enforced medical option, to say nothing of the cost.
- The recommended solution is to do an exploratory exorcism. In my experience, clients with serious mental health issues do not manifest when the Rite is prayed over them. In this case, you leave it at that and don't invite them back for further sessions. I doubt that one or two sessions of the exorcism prayer would be harmful but any more than that could be. Further sessions would delay their getting the treatment they need and might, in some cases, foster delusional thinking.
- Of course, if evidence of serious mental health problems or the likelihood thereof surfaces in the initial interview, you don't do even an exploratory exorcism. You ask them to get a letter from their doctor or psychologist giving the OK for exorcism prayers. It's unlikely that you will hear anything back from the medico.

What you look for in the initial interview is evidence of previous diagnoses of serious mental health problems and/or of on-going treatment or medication for such. Another clue is in any letter or email sent by the client to the exorcist. If it is of considerable length, doubts are raised. If it doesn't quite make logical sense as a coherent whole or if it contains bizarre images of things seen and heard (especially that), you should check out the person's medical history.

The psychological approach focuses on uncovering mental health issues; it does not reveal if a person is possessed. For that, a further step is needed namely an exploratory exorcism. In the last case described by Mgr Rossetti (above), the final step is to pray over the client 'and see how she reacts'. I think this means doing an exploratory exorcism over the person. Could this final step replace the need for a psychological examination? I believe so. In my experience, as already stated, people with serious mental health issues don't usually manifest, that is, react under the recitation of the Rite. If you can get a psychologist on the team, well and good but if not, the exorcist can proceed with an exploratory exorcism after questioning the client about their mental health history.

THE EXPLORATORY EXORCISM

The fourth approach to discernment of spirits involves actually doing an exorcism over the person. When first appointed as exorcist I prayed the rite of exorcism over everyone who came and told them to come back next week if that helped. I thought that is what an exorcist did. Clearly, there was no future in doing that if only because my diary was soon overflowing. One thing I learnt from that initial period was that while most did not react some, a small minority did. They manifested.

In a few cases it was frightening; in all cases intriguing. It turned out that, for the most part, these were the people I was able to help. The conclusion I drew was that the best way of discerning the need for an exorcism came by means of doing an exorcism, what I call the 'exploratory exorcism'. That has been my experience. When I started to read some experts on the subject, I found that my two favourite authors, Chenesseau[30] and Amorth, had long been teaching this very same approach.

Amorth writes: 'This is the problem: in order to ascertain the presence of a possession with a certain margin of security, the best diagnostic instrument is the exorcism itself. In brief, without performing the exorcism, it is difficult to determine if there is truly need of it'.[31] Amorth found support for this view in the writings of the 8th century theologian Alcuin 'which also grants the exorcism a diagnostic purpose'.[32] Does it matter if the exorcist got it wrong and the exploratory exorcism showed up nothing? Fr Amorth (2016) answers: 'Let us just say an exorcism does no one any harm'.[33]

Fr Chenesseau[34] also favours the exploratory exorcism. He doesn't use the term but suggests that when there is doubt about the signs and symptoms of possession showing up in the life of a person, 'which happens in the majority of cases, it is preferable to do an exorcism'.[35] He

---

30 *Journal d'un Prêtre Exorciste*, p. 229.
31 *An Exorcist Explains the Demonic*, p. 99.
32 Ibid., p. 100.
33 Ibid., p. 101.
34 *Journal d'un Prêtre Exorciste*, p. 229.
35 Ibid., p. 262.

compares an exorcism done in these circumstances to a doctor doing exploratory surgery.

The question then becomes, what is it that happens during the performance of an exorcism that gives, if not absolute certainty, at least a much greater degree of confidence that a person is possessed? It is the phenomenon about which we have already spoken, called *manifestation*. If the client over whom you are praying the Rite manifests during the prayer, you invite that person back for further prayer. Thus, you begin the process of exorcism which may involve many sessions lasting weeks, months, or in some cases years. In each session you repeat the prayers of the Rite.

Summary

The best way, I believe, of discerning whether someone has an evil spirit or not is to combine two of the above discernment methods, 'signs and symptoms' and the 'exploratory exorcism'. I look for evidence of pain, sorrow, misery in a person's life which is not easily explained along with feelings of hatred towards God and holy things. If satisfied on these points, I will do an exploratory exorcism.

Often, however, the genuinely possessed have difficulty in describing what is happening to them. You need to take this into account. Too much detail, and long, convoluted stories, on the other hand, are more often evidence of mental problems or a lively imagination.

There is a degree of subjectivity in making such judgments and some exorcists will be harder to convince than others. With experience, the exorcist gets better at assessing candidates.

Chapter Eight

More on 'manifestation'

In the approach to exorcism being proposed here, the best way of discerning the presence of evil spirits is through 'manifestation'. This term refers to the strange even bizarre behaviour that sometimes occurs during the praying of the Rite of Exorcism over a person. Such behaviour may include screaming, yelling, shaking, blaspheming, cursing, vomiting, falling to the floor, fainting, etc. Sometimes it can be violent and frightening.

I have always taken this sort of behaviour – occurring during the prayer of exorcism – as the clearest sign of the presence of a demon. It is not absolutely certain and the exorcist should retain a certain degree of scepticism even in front of the most extreme behaviour of this kind. However, I believe it is the strongest evidence of demonic possession we have. If none of this behaviour occurs during an exorcism – as is most often the case – I think we can conclude the person is not possessed. Some clarification of the nature and the description of 'manifestation' may be in order.

During the prayer

'Manifestation' as possible evidence of an evil spirit presence refers to the strange behaviours that can occur during the recitation of the Rite of Exorcism over a person. People who come seeking help often speak of bizarre, frightening, or devilish-type behaviour occurring at times or indeed often in the day-to-day life of the person purportedly possessed. That's why they have approached the exorcist. If, however, on doing an exploratory exorcism, the person remains completely still without reacting in any way at all, you can reasonably conclude that the strange behaviour is not due to evil spirit possession. Some family members can react negatively to this diagnosis, accusing the exorcist of incompetence. Stick to your guns.

There is one exception to this rule: sometimes an afflicted person turns up at the front door already manifesting. The devil knows what's coming. Bring them in and pray the Rite of Exorcism over them. The manifestation should continue, diminishing in intensity if not in that first session, at least over subsequent sessions.

Can it be faked?

Yes, of course. People have seen the films, read the books. With experience you get better at identifying theatrics. As a rule, they are very loud and produce exaggerated gestures and facial grimaces. It comes over as slightly amusing. Authentic manifestations can be loud and 'over the top' too, so don't rush to judgment, but there is nothing amusing in the spectacle. The sheer hatred often present in the eyes of those genuinely afflicted is difficult to emulate and spine chilling. A surer sign of invention is in the utterances allegedly coming from the demon. If they are lengthy and overly articulate, you should have doubts.

One client I had would give a running commentary during the prayer on how well I was doing. He would say: 'Ouch, that hurt, yes, he's doing well, but he is not good enough to get me out'. It could have been true, but demons are usually not so articulate. In the exorcisms I have performed, demonic utterances have been few and always raspy and guttural mutterings of 'I'm not going' – all the more threatening for being barely audible.

Fr Amorth agrees with this point of view: 'Some believe, I know not why, that demons are talkative and that, if they are present during an exorcism, the demon will publicly denounce all their sins. It is a false belief; demons are reluctant to speak'.[36] However, he admits there are exceptions and tells of a sceptical priest who was present at one of his exorcisms. The demon turned to the priest and said, 'You say that you don't believe that I exist. But you believe in women; yes, you believe in women, and how!' Mercifully, this is not common.

A surer sign of an authentic manifestation occurs when the persons manifesting – in addition to bizarre behaviour – seem to withdraw into a world of their own. They might hiss at the exorcist and even take a swipe in his direction, but apart from that seem to be not quite in

---

36 *An Exorcist Tells His Story*, p. 94.

touch with their immediate surroundings. Towards the end of the session you notice them coming out of that withdrawn state; sometimes you have to call them back out of it, saying things like – 'That's enough, come back now', or 'OK, that's it. We're finished now'. They quickly return to the present time and place. With experience, you get better at identifying authentic manifestations.

However, the surest way to deal with fakers and fantasists is the modus operandi being proposed here. You do an exploratory exorcism. If there is manifestation during the prayer, you invite the person to return for further sessions. You expect the strength of the manifestation to diminish, albeit slowly, over subsequent sessions. If, after a decent number of sessions, there is no lessening of intensity you let the person go. Either the demon is too strong, there is a mental sickness, or the person is making it up. With a performance, the script usually doesn't change.

Psychosis

A more serious question is whether manifestation is some sort of psychotic episode. The sudden onset of a 'manifestation' – usually early in an exorcism – is arresting and can be alarming. The person seems to be out of control, their behaviour far from normal. A few points can be made which do, I think, clearly distinguish a 'manifestation' especially of a violent kind from symptoms of a psychotic episode:

More on 'manifestation'

- The 'manifestation' is usually highly focused. The understanding is that in 'manifestations' the demon takes over the person's body and acts through it or with it. As a result, the body of the person shows great anger, and the eyes are filled with hatred towards the exorcist who is commanding it to go in name of Christ. The demon doesn't want to go and resists in ugly ways. This is not irrational. It makes good sense. The demon doesn't want to go back to hell.
- Generally, the manifestations begin at the start of the exorcism prayer and taper out as it draws to a close. The exorcist can even hasten the closure by calling to the person 'underneath' to 'come back now', 'that's enough', etc. The nice person at the start of the session gradually resurfaces. Psychoses are not of such short duration.
- If the 'manifestations' are due to an evil spirit, they should keep lessening in intensity over subsequent sessions. If they do not, there is some other explanation. One such would be mental sickness in which case the prayers of exorcism should be terminated.

When I began work as an exorcist, I had a fear of sparking a psychotic episode in the person I was praying over. It has never happened. Attention to the medical history of the person should obviate the danger. If there is a history of severe mental health issues, don't do an exorcism. Otherwise, if the person suddenly bursts forth in a frightening manifestation, you remain as calm as possible and just keep praying the prescribed prayers.

Unconscious

Some authors say that a lapse into unconsciousness under the prayer of exorcism is the only true manifestation of an evil spirit presence. Fr Poulain, for example, writes 'in the strict sense of the word, ... a person is possessed by the Devil when at particular moments the Devil makes him lose consciousness...'.[37] If this does not happen, according to Poulain, the person is obsessed (or oppressed as I would say) but not possessed. In my experience falling unconscious during an exorcism is but one symptom or manifestation of demonic presence. There can be many others equally valid. Fr Chenesseau would seem to agree: 'For the possessed, a lapse of consciousness usually takes place during exorcism. This starts with the first prayers. The person who a minute before was conversing quite normally is suddenly overcome by a kind of sleep *or on the contrary* becomes agitated and transformed in appearance, his eyes are fixed and haggard. Another spirit has substituted itself in his body'.[38]

Falling asleep or becoming unconscious can be a symptom of 'manifestation' but so too can the sudden onset of bizarre behaviour and change in facial appearance. I have found the latter type of manifestation more common. However, while not falling asleep or becoming unconscious, it's possible the person 'manifesting' under the prayer may not be fully aware of what is happening.

---

[37] *The Graces of Interior Prayer*, p. 428.
[38] *Journal d'un Prêtre Exorciste*, p. 296. Italics are mine, not in the original.

Chapter Nine

Miscellanea

This chapter attempts to tie up some loose ends and to give greater clarity on issues that have already been touched upon.

SCHIZOPHRENIA

It is better not to pray the Rite over people with serious mental health issues, especially those involving delusional thinking. Clients with schizophrenia present a special challenge for the exorcist since the symptoms such as 'hearing voices' are not always disclosed. These people can approach an exorcist, asking for an exorcism, believing their symptoms are demonic in origin.

The exorcist should ask prospective clients if they have had any serious mental health problems such as schizophrenia or if they hear voices. They may not answer honestly or may claim that the diagnosis was wrong which, although unlikely, could be true. In either case, the best response it to pray the Rite over them by way of an exploratory exorcism. In my experience, clients with serious mental health problems, such as schizophrenia, do not manifest under the prayer. Hence, there are no more sessions.

Could exorcism be harmful to these people?

Since it is essentially a prayer, I don't believe the Rite of Exorcism is in itself harmful as long as it is done as the Church prescribes with voice only and no physical manipulation of the client. However, harm could be done to a schizophrenic sufferer if the prayer were repeated often over subsequent sessions. This would prevent the client from getting the treatment needed, and might also foster the delusional thinking associated with the disorder. (Only once, in my experience, did a client with schizophrenia manifest. In that case, however, the manifestation did not decrease over subsequent sessions. The process was soon stopped.)

Schizophrenic clients occasionally insist that you continue to pray for them across subsequent sessions, claiming the prayers are helping them. You could ask that they get a letter from their doctor giving permission for the exorcism prayers to continue. No response – the most likely – would indicate a negative answer.

Male and female

Most schizophrenics that I have encountered have been in their twenties, and female. A smaller number were middle-aged men. The latter described attacks by Satan on their persons usually of a sexual nature. Not only did they not manifest during the exploratory exorcism but in the following session their symptoms had worsened and they described them even more graphically. Don't proceed any further with these clients but insist they see a doctor or psychiatrist. Their symptoms seem seriously psychotic.

How can we help?

We should not shun people with serious mental health issues who come for the exorcist's help. They are sufferers who need our compassion. Instead of the Rite of Exorcism, however, there would be prayers of support, healing and simple deliverance, all the while insisting they undergo medical treatment and keep to the medication prescribed. Unfortunately, there is a limit on the number of such clients an exorcist can handle since they tend to be on-going. Support from parish prayer groups and similar ministries could be called upon to help with these cases.

COUPLE MINISTRY

Exorcism is a one-on-one ministry. Sometimes, however, I have prayed over married couples together. Their spiritual life can be so integrated that any evil spirit attacking one also affects the other. More complicated is the situation when a spouse, usually the wife, says the husband has got the devil in him. If she offers serious evidence of it, and you think it justified, you could pray the Rite over her. You would not repeat the prayer often and if any domestic violence were involved, you would urge her to report it.

A similar and not uncommon situation is when a parent, usually a mother, describes a teenage daughter as 'off the planet' with rebellion and hatred. Teachers, doctors and psychologists are involved but the hatred seems to continue. In these cases, I have prayed the Rite over the mother a few times. There is little doubt Satan is in the mix. The prayer seems to help calm these situations. Sometimes, I have been asked to pray the Rite for adult sons or daughters but I usually refuse. Adults must ask for help themselves.

The Rite of Exorcism is a powerful prayer. It's mainly for possession but can, I think, be used in other situations in which Satan is involved. These situations are called 'oppression' and when they cause great distress, you can, I believe, use the Rite of Exorcism praying over the sufferer a few times; but not (as described in chapter 5) where the cause of the distress is a bodily sickness, or of purely mental origin, for example, schizophrenia or obsessive thoughts.

MORE ON PSYCHOLOGY

Some of the best outcomes I have had as an exorcist have been with people who presented with a clean bill of health from psychiatrists. They came to me concluding that since there was no medical explanation for their troubling behaviour or feelings, they must be due to evil spirits. In some cases, this has turned out to be true. But not always. There may be issues that have been missed by the psychiatric testing, such as personality disorders, mood disorders, or broken down and toxic relationships. The absence of any major mental health disorder does not prove that Satan is responsible for strange or troubling behaviour in a person. It could be, but not always, not often.

A defence mechanism

It could also be that some clients use Satan or possession by evil spirits – unconsciously for the most part – as some sort of defence mechanism against facing unpleasant truths. It puts the problem 'out there' and diverts attention from the real issue. I suspect there are some who would rather believe they are under attack from Satan than admit to any mental or emotional disorder.

When the exorcist finds no evidence of evil spirit possession (usually through an exploratory exorcism), these clients sometimes get angry. They may accuse the exorcist of incompetence or even say he is a false priest. My response is to say I'm sorry but I can't be further involved.

WITCHCRAFT AND THE OCCULT

A frequent request for help comes from people who complain of constant bad luck in their lives or of a string of costly and dangerous incidents continuing to afflict them. When asked 'What do you think is causing this?', they inevitably attribute the problem to someone who has placed a curse, a hex, or a magic spell upon them. They clearly believe what they are saying and often exhibit fear and anxiety. As a rule, I tend to take these people seriously given the massive rise in the cult of witchcraft and other forms of occult involvement in the western world today, even among Catholics.

After questioning these people about their lives and the extent of their Catholic faith and practice, I usually do an exploratory exorcism. If they manifest, there are more sessions. But, even if no manifestation occurs, I repeat the Rite a number of times, praying against 'oppression' since they have opened themselves to demonic influence. Christian counselling may be needed as well, since occult involvement – with its belief in curses, spells, sorceries and so on – can create a mentality steeped in anxiety and fear. They need to be taught to have radical trust in Jesus, that our lives and future are totally in his hands.

Catholics who have been into witchcraft should also be urged to go to Confession in case there was some intentional cooperation in occult practices. These are sins against the First Commandment and need to be repented of. (Witchcraft may be a situation where the use of the Rite of Exorcism to free people is limited to practising Christians. Others are likely to see exorcism as just another magic formula.)

RESTRAINT (Do you tie them up?)

This is one of the most sensitive issues in the ministry of exorcism. Should you tie a person up before starting an exorcism or perhaps during it? Very definitely, the answer is no! You could be breaking the law if you do so.

Although not occurring very often, I have experienced manifestations of a violent and threatening kind. The look in these clients' eyes was of sheer hatred and their bodily posture extremely unsettling. Apart from sending the assistant out of the room and keeping out of range of the person's hands or feet, you just keep on praying the prescribed prayer. Towards the end of the exorcism session, the person calms down and returns, albeit groggily, to normal. In subsequent sessions, you would expect the severity of the manifestation to gradually reduce. Keep in mind that the hatred being expressed is not against the exorcist himself but against Christ who is the one really doing the exorcism. Have faith in Our Lord that he will protect you. I also pray to Our Lady in these circumstances.

The thought of restraining a client rarely arises, but it can. It's a dangerous path. In Australia, some clients have died during exorcisms (not done under Catholic auspices) with those responsible subsequently charged with manslaughter.[39] In all such cases the clients had been restrained in some way, although improper manhandling of the client was probably more at fault then the restraint itself.

---

39 Trove: Exorcism.

PRAYER AND PREVENTION

Clients are asked not to pray during the session. (It could hide signs of 'manifestation'.) Leave the praying to the exorcist. But clients should be encouraged to pray between sessions as much as they are able. I give them a booklet by Archbishop Porteus, *Prayers for those Experiencing Spiritual Affliction*.[40]

The aim and purpose of Catholic exorcism is not just to free people from Satanic attack but to help them find God and a deeper union with him. Adam C. Blai recommends a balanced Catholic life as the best preventative measures against infection or reinfection by demonic spirits. These include:

- 'Participating in the sacramental life. For lay people this means Baptism, Confirmation and Reconciliation, as well as the Eucharist on Sunday and holy days.

- 'Remaining in the state of grace. This means avoiding mortal sin and repenting of mortal sin when we do not avoid it.

- 'Maintaining a balanced and healthy prayer life... (comprising) prayers of praise, petition for ourselves, intercession for others, and thanksgiving to God.

---

40 *Prayers for those Experiencing Spiritual Affliction*. 2012. London: Catholic Truth Society.

- 'Developing a proper understanding of the spiritual world and becoming educated in spiritual and religious matters (catechesis)... (This) removes the fear-based idea that demons are free to do as they wish.

- 'Making use of sacramentals and blessings. Homes should be blessed thoroughly... Holy water and blessed salt should be in the homes and used as needed. A blessed holy symbol, perhaps a crucifix, should be prominent in every room. A consecration of the home to the Sacred Heart of Jesus and the Immaculate Heart of Mary... (but) it should only be done if all the family members are in agreement.'[41]

I would also emphasise the need for scripture reading as a part of our daily spiritual routine as well as the recitation of the rosary. The Word of God and devotion to Our Lady are very powerful defences against the wiles of Satan. Of course, while an exorcist priest can command Satan to leave a person, he can only invite that person to convert to a radically Christ-centred lifestyle.

OVERLOAD

The most enduring challenge of the exorcist ministry is that of discernment. How do you know if a prospective client is truly under extraordinary attack by Satan or demons? Discernment is not an exact science. Even with

---

[41] *Hauntings, Possessions and Exorcisms*, pp. 74-75.

the approach advocated here – that of the exploratory exorcism – the end result could well be too many unnecessary exorcisms. That may not matter very much since, as Fr Amorth said, 'An unnecessary exorcism never hurt anyone'.[42] But, it could become a growing burden for the exorcist and one most likely to take him out of the ministry. Some guidelines would be helpful.

Care needs to be taken, however, that requirements are not set too high. Putting a prospective client on a lengthy prayer program, as proposed in one Australian diocese, seems senseless. One of the symptoms of demonic possession or oppression is often a disgust for prayer and holy things. This proposal could weed out some who most need the exorcist's prayers.

Another proposal to help separate the sheep from the goats is to have an independent committee do the discernment. This raises not only the question of privacy – they would have to know all the personal details of the case – but also the need to have the exorcist priest involved in the discernment process. Some evil spirits only show themselves when the Rite is prayed over the sufferer. No doubt, the exorcist could benefit from the help of others in the discernment process – a psychologist on the team, for example, if you can get one. But to farm out that process to others *in toto* seems a mistake.

Some preliminary screening by an associate of the exorcist would save him from unnecessary work. There

---

[42] *An Exorcist tells his Story*, p. 45.

are some mental health situations where exorcism is not advised, some religious belief systems incompatible with Christianity, and, of course, some people who don't need an exorcism (the mentally handicapped, for example). Co-workers in the exorcism ministry can be trained to recognise these cases. There are also clients who keep returning for more of the same and others who go from exorcist to exorcist. These could be gently dissuaded without reference to the exorcist. Overall, however, the exorcist should be involved in the discernment process and, preferably, be the one to make the final decision to proceed or not.

There are questions as to how open and accessible to the public the exorcist and his ministry should be. I don't think we should advertise but neither should we hide behind excessive church regulations and a veil of holy obscurantism. If Catholics want to see an exorcist, they should have a reasonable chance of doing so. Of course, the obvious measure to prevent overload would be to appoint more priests to the ministry.

Summaries

Chapter Ten

Security

The following are some issues of security. There may be more, but these are important.

Man of prayer

You don't have to be a saint, but you need to be a man of God, a man of prayer. Our adversary the devil will exploit any serious moral weakness we might have. In the Catholic Church, only priests appointed by the bishop may exercise the ministry of exorcism. While that can seriously restrict the ministry, it is also a powerful protection for the priest so appointed and for the one seeking exorcism. It underscores that the one doing the exorcism is Christ in his mystical body, the church. The exorcist is only the instrument in his hands and, as such, not Satan's primary focus.

Never alone

Some say the exorcist should have a team with him. It is often impractical but also raises privacy issues. I can't imagine that many would want an audience at their exorcism. It is better, I think, to have one assistant, a number on call perhaps, but only one at each exorcism.

It's better the assistant be a woman of mature faith and discretion, and not likely to be frightened too much by manifestations should they appear. The assistant may be invited to pray during the exorcism but must never say the prayers of the Rite.

No physical contact

Apart from laying hands gently and momentarily on the head, and putting a stole around the shoulders, there must be no other physical contact with persons being exorcised. You must never hit, beat, shake or mistreat them in any way. You may raise the voice somewhat when addressing the demon but avoid undue theatricality. The power is in the prayer. It's Our Lord speaking. We can hardly improve on that. If the client is a woman and she falls to the floor while manifesting, the assistant should put a blanket over her.

Minors

Never pray over a minor without a parent also being present. With a teenager, make sure s/he wants it. It may be just mum's idea. Mum may be right, but you can't do an exorcism without the candidate's free assent. With this proviso, I have prayed for exorcism over teenagers but never over a child (age 13 or under) and would be very hesitant to do so. In such cases, you would always defer to doctors or child psychologists.

Sometimes, a client comes accompanied by family members. If it's a case of suspected possession, and therefore a true exorcism, send children or vulnerable adults out of the room; manifestations can be frightening. If it's a case of vexation this is not a concern since there is no manifestation. Sometimes a parent comes with a child implying that the child is the one being vexed when it is really the parent with the problem. Sit them down and pray over both together.

Length of time

A session of exorcism shouldn't last longer than an hour at the most and usually less than that. I suggest half an hour. If at the end of a session more is needed, invite them back same time, same place, next week. It seems that most cases where exorcists have ended up in the hands of the law, the exorcism session went on for hours if not days.

Restraint

Some authors recommend clients be tied to a chair or held down by others. Manifestations during an exorcism can indeed be frightening and threatening. However, I think it important that we avoid these measures. Send the assistant out of the room, stand back, but otherwise keep praying the Rite. Personally, I have never tied a client up even though I have been frightened at times.

It's a more difficult situation if a client turns up restrained by relatives, and already manifesting. I suggest that the exorcist bring them all in and start praying the prayer while asking the relatives to release their grip. In any further sessions, you would not have the relatives present. The rule is that no one is to be subjected to the exorcism prayer against their will.

Obsessive thoughts

Don't pray the Rite over anyone with suicidal ideas or who has obsessive thoughts about harming others. Leave these cases to doctors and psychologists.

Money

Catholic exorcists don't charge anything. Nor should gift giving be encouraged.

Doctors

Catholic exorcists respect the medical profession. If someone is under treatment by a psychiatrist or a psychologist for a serious mental health condition, don't go there. You may pray prayers of support and healing but not exorcism. If the person keeps insisting, tell them to get a letter from their doctor authorising an exorcism. You are unlikely to hear from the person again.

As a general principle, don't do an exorcism over people who have had or are likely to have had a diagnosis of a serious mental health condition. We need to remember that possession by a demon is a rare condition, mental sickness is not.

Take notes

The exorcist should take some notes. I note down the client's first name and the date and time of the visit. Telephone numbers are in my diary entry. Brief notes are made to indicate the nature of the problem, any manifestations, and improvement, if any, over subsequent sessions. Note also who was present, including the assistant. For quick access, the use of a card index system is preferable.

Death by exorcism

There have been instances of people dying under exorcism. We can learn from these cases.

1. One of the most infamous cases occurred in rural Victoria in January 1993, performed by a Pentecostal group. Mrs Joan Vollmer underwent an exorcism ceremony during which she was subjected to pressure on her stomach and chest in an attempt to force the evil spirits out of her. She was also tied to a chair during the exorcism which had lasted for four hours when she died, reportedly from internal injuries. Her

husband, and three other people – the exorcists – were charged with manslaughter but acquitted in a trial in late 1993.[43] The reason for the acquittal was insufficient evidence that the exorcists' activities had caused her death. But there was another trial a year later. This time the husband and three exorcists were convicted of 'recklessly causing injury and false imprisonment'. Sentences were reduced to two and three months for two of the exorcists and suspended for the husband and the third exorcist.[44]

The lessons are clear: Don't subject the person being exorcised to duress of any kind; don't let a session of exorcism continue for more than an hour at the most; and, think very carefully before restraining the person. It is also evident that little attention was paid to the lady's physical or mental health beforehand.

2. The second case occurred under Catholic auspices in Germany in 1976. A young woman, Annaliese Michel, was exorcised over a long period involving sixty-nine sessions in total. She died after the sixty-ninth and the priest exorcists were subsequently tried and convicted of responsibility for her death.

At first sight, it seems that everything was done correctly, all the boxes were ticked. The bishop gave his approval, two senior priests were appointed to be the exorcists, medical opinion was sought, the young

---

43 *The Canberra Times*, 17 September 1993, Trove, p. 2.
44 *The Canberra Times*, 2 December 1994, Trove, p. 4.

woman was not restrained nor put under duress in any way, the sessions were not overly long and, most importantly, she manifested during the performance of the rite. What went wrong?

One opinion is that Annaliese was chosen by God to be a suffering soul and that's why the exorcism did not work[45] and she died in the process. Another possible view is that serious errors were made by the exorcists concerned:

a. *They took insufficient notice of the medical opinion.* Annaliese herself was adamant that mental health was not the problem. In this she was supported by her mother. This is not an unusual situation. The exorcist must resist such pressure. Only doctors should diagnose.

b. *The manifestation continued unabated.* If a manifestation is truly from a demon it should weaken in intensity over subsequent sessions. If there is no sign of such a change over a decent interval (seven or eight sessions) the exorcism should not continue. In the case of Annaliese there was at least one manifestation that continued throughout the exorcism process – she kept giving sharp, articulate messages purportedly from the demons. According to Fr Amorth,[46] this would be a highly

---

45 Jose Antonio Fortea and Lawrence E. U. LeBlanc. *Anneliese Michel: A True Story of a Case of Demonic Possession – Germany 1976.* 2012. E-book edition.

46 *An Exorcist Tells his Story*, p. 94.

unusual and therefore unlikely form of demonic manifestation. Whatever about that, the messages kept coming across the sixty-nine sessions. The exorcism should have been abandoned long before that number was reached. Whether Annaliese was a chosen, suffering soul or whether it was all part of a psychosis, there was clearly risk in continuing the exorcism with no change in the main manifestation.

c. *Her health was in decline.* Fr. Chenesseau[47] says that proof that persons have a demon and are being healed by the exorcism prayers is seen in their improvement in health. Fearing the placebo effect, I would place more emphasis on the lessening of the manifestation across subsequent sessions. Nevertheless, the health of clients is important. Often, I have found that clients do indeed show improvement in health and well-being. However, it's of more importance that their health does not worsen. As the sessions went on, Annaliese's health began to decline. Evidently, she was not eating. The exorcism should have been abandoned as soon as her failing health was noted.

d. *They listened to the demons.* One of the messages given through Annaliese was that the demons would leave on a certain date. It is possible the priests continued the sessions longer than

---

[47] *Journal d'un Prêtre Exorciste*, p. 61.

advisable because of this message. The exorcist should never enter into dialogue with demons or be influenced by anything they say. They are agents of Satan, the father and prince of lies. On the said date, some demons left but others did not. Even then, they continued with the exorcism sessions for another month when Annaliese tragically died.

One to one

Exorcism is mainly a one to one ministry. There is no such thing as a 'general exorcism' or exorcism of a group of people at once. In the 16th and 17th centuries, there were epidemics of 'possession' with people falling into trances and cavorting about with grotesque distortions, wild gesticulations and acrobatic exploits. The story is graphically told in Jean Lhermitte's book *True or False Possession* first published, in French, in 1956.[48] There was even a convent of nuns so afflicted to the scandal of many. According to Lhermitte (2013, English translation) it was due largely to mass hysteria, or 'the mental contagion of the weak-minded'.[49] Individuals can falsely believe they are possessed by demons, and for that reason an exorcist should always maintain a degree of scepticism. But when the manifestations or demon-like behaviour happen in a

---

48 *True or False Possession: How to Distinguish the Demonic from the Demented.*
49 Ibid., p. 64.

group setting, the scepticism should be total. Leave such to doctors and psychologists.

Burn out

If he is not careful, an exorcist can soon have a long list of people who have become permanently attached to his ministrations. Often, it seems to me, people who have been freed of evil spirits don't stay around. Perhaps it's because possession or even oppression were painful, even embarrassing experiences. The people who do tend to stay around, returning for more of the same prayer were not possessed. They liked the prayer, perhaps felt its power. But the ritual of exorcism is not meant for on-going prayer support. The first motive of the exorcist should be to help people, the second to protect himself from unreasonable requests and burn out.

Freelancers Beware

Christian exorcism is based on the belief that it is Christ our Lord who is the exorcist. We are but instruments in his hands. Thus, all exorcisms are done in the name and with the power of Christ. This is evident in the Ritual itself. Of course, anyone can claim to be exorcising in the name of Christ and may even use a pirated copy of the Ritual. It is only appointment by the bishop to the office of exorcist that guarantees we are indeed ministers of Christ. A passage from Acts of the Apostles tells of seven men who took it upon themselves to exorcise 'by the Jesus whom Paul proclaims'. The evil spirit attacked them saying, 'Jesus I know, and Paul I know but who are you?' (see Acts 19:13-16).

Chapter Eleven

Dealing with a client

1 First contact (by phone email or letter).
You make an appointment.
(Even at this stage, you might see reasons for not proceeding.)

2 First session (in your office or place of prayer).
Gentle questioning of the client. You seek to discover:

a. any serious reason against proceeding
b. any indication that an evil spirit might be present

If answer to a) is 'no' and b) 'yes', take the next step.

3 Do an exploratory exorcism (usually during the first session if there is time left after the questioning. Otherwise, make an appointment for another session).

4 The next step depends on what happened during the exploratory exorcism.

(A) **Nothing happens, there is no manifestation.**
Tell the client that there is no indication of an evil spirit present in their soul. Make no further appointments.[50]

---

[50] Clients who don't manifest are prayed over with the Rite of Exorcism only once. However, if you think it's a case of **'oppression'** or **'vexation'**, you invite them back for further sessions. With **'oppression'**,

(B) **The client manifests.**
You invite the person to return next week for another session in which the Rite of Exorcism is repeated. You continue to do this until the manifestations have ceased or largely so. It may be weeks, months, or even years.

Caveat. If the manifestations in (B) do not change and weaken in intensity after about eight sessions (or sooner in some cases), you bring the exorcism process to a halt. Something else is happening. Sometimes there might be an initial increase in intensity but over time that should change. With some long-term clients the change can be very slow and subtle, and seem to stop for a while, but over time it is evident. It is up to the exorcist's judgment to decide when enough is enough.

---

you continue with further sessions while the life-crisis is at its height; with 'vexation', you continue as long as the sessions produce improvement. Fairly soon they will stop coming – they are healed.

Chapter Twelve

Using the ritual

Suggestions

Using the 1998 Ritual

a. Pray a decade of the rosary, then read a selection of the preliminary invocations, prayers, litanies, psalms, Gospel readings. The selection is taken from paragraphs 39-58 in the Ritual. (More are found in sections 57-80.) Only a selection is used. This part of the session should last no more than ten minutes. A binding prayer against Satan[51] is also recommended for inclusion in the opening prayers.
b. The 'Exorcismi formulae' are then read. I say one 'formula deprecativa' (61) and two or three of the 'formula imperativa' (62, 82, 84) which are repeated if time permits.
c. The session concludes with a selection of closing prayers (63-65).[52] An anointing may also be given on the forehead and hands using not the oil of the sick but oil blessed by the priest.

---

51 See Appendix to this chapter. *
52 See Appendix to this chapter. **

The 1614 Ritual

Some clients ask for the old ritual in Latin. If using it I don't read the section at the beginning commanding the demon to reveal its name and date of departure. This is not in the new ritual and could encourage the exorcist to enter into some sort of dialogue with Satan, 'the father and prince of lies'.

A combination of both rituals

My own practice is to use a combination of the old and new rituals. I have an English translation of the old 1614 ritual which I recite largely in full, apart from the above mentioned section that interrogates the demon. Included are the opening prayers, litanies, and scripture readings and then a selection of exorcism prayers of which there are several. After that, I read two or three of 'imperativa' prayers from the new ritual in Latin.

Appendix

* A binding prayer asks God to protect all present against reprisal acts by the demons being cast out. A number of such prayers are found in 'Deliverance Prayers' by Fr Chad Ripperger.[53]

---

[53] *Deliverance Prayers. For use by the laity.* 2016. Sensus Traditionis Press.

Using the ritual

** I like to finish the exorcism session with a prayer given me by the late Fr John Shanley of the Diocese of Sale. The prayer asks God to heal any damage, scars or unhealthy inclinations left in the soul after the demon's expulsion. Although never an official exorcist, Fr John had a marvellous deliverance ministry in his rural parish. People came by bus from all over Victoria and N.S.W. to attend his monthly healing and deliverance Mass.

Dear Jesus through the power of Your Precious Blood, I break and dissolve any curse, hex, seal, spell, sorcery, bond, snare, pact, trap or device, lie, stumbling block, obstacle, deception, diversion, distraction, spiritual chain, or malign spiritual influence placed upon (...) by any person or thing associated with Satan or other occult powers.

Also, through the power of Your Precious Blood, I break and dissolve any dysfunction, derangement or any disorder of body, soul, mind and spirit placed upon (....) by any person, or thing associated with Satan or occult powers.

I also break and dissolve any bondage put upon (...) be it through the agency of demonic spirits, coven of witches or warlocks, groups of Satan cultists, chanters of satanic rituals or offices or anything brought upon (....) by his/her own mistakes or sins, or by traumatic experiences earlier in life.

Bibliography

AMORTH, FR GABRIELE. (1999). *An Exorcist Tells His Story.* San Francisco: Ignatius Press.

AMORTH, FR GABRIELE, with Stimamiglio, Stefano. (2016). *An Exorcist Explains the Demonic.* Manchester, NH: Sophia Institute Press.

AMORTH, FR GABRIELE, with Fezzi, Elisabetta. (2017). *My Battle Against Satan.* Manchester, NH. Sophia Institute Press.

CANBERRA TIMES (1993). In www.trove.nia.gov.au/newspapers&magazines/exorcism p. 2. 'Court clears four after exorcism death.'

CANBERRA TIMES (1994). In www.trove.nia.gov.au/newspapers&magazines/exorcism p. 4. 'Two jailed for role in fatal exorcism ritual.'

CHENESSEAU, PÈRE RENÉ (2007). *Journal d'un Prêtre Exorciste.* Rome: Editions Nova Millenium Romae.

BLAI, ADAM. C. (2017). *Hauntings, Possessions, and Exorcisms.* Steubenville, Ohio: Emmaus Road Publishing.

DAVIES, FR JEREMY, (2009). *Exorcism. Understanding exorcism in scripture and practice.* London: Catholic Truth Society.

FORTEA, FR JOSE ANTONIO & LAWRENCE E. U. LEBLANC (2012). *Anneliese Michel. A true story of a case of demonic possession*, Germany 1976. eBook publication.

LHERMITTE, JEAN. (2013). *True or False Possession? How to Distinguish the Demonic from the Demented.* Manchester, NH. Sophia Institute Press.

POULAIN, FR A, S.J. (1978 edition). *The Graces of Interior Prayer. A Treatise on Mystical Theology.* Vermont: Celtic Cross Books.

PORTEUS, BISHOP JULIAN. (2012). *Prayers for those experiencing Spiritual Affliction.* London: Catholic Truth Society.

RIPPERGER, FR CHAD. *Deliverance Prayers. For use by the Laity.* Sensus Traditionis Press.

RITUAL (1614). *De Exorcizandis Obsessis a Daemonio.* Old Roman Ritual.

RITUAL (1998). *De Exorcismis et Supplicationibus quibusdam.* Vatican: Congregation for Divine Worship.

ROSSETTI, FR STEPHEN JOSEPH (2021). *Diary of an American Exorcist. Demons, Possession, and the Modern-Day Battle against Ancient Evil.* Manchester: NH. Sophia Institute Press.

TROVE. www.trove.nia.gov.au/newspapers&magazines/Exorcism

www.ingramcontent.com/pod-product-compliance
Lightning Source LLC
Chambersburg PA
CBHW012006090526
44590CB00026B/3895